Linh Dao & Pavla Hanáčková

WHY KANGAROOS HAVE POCKETS

HOW ANIMALS CARE FOR THEIR YOUNG

Australian
GEOGRAPHIC

Table of contents

ANIMAL CHILDHOOD

Have you ever wondered what it's like for animals to be young? How their parents take care of them so that they are safe from enemies, and at the same time learn everything they need to know? Some animal babies are like human babies, defenceless and dependent on the care provided by adults. Mammals rank as the most attentive parents because they feed their young with milk, but fish, reptile, amphibian, bird and insect species also have some diligent parents. And by the same token, you can find some mammals who don't look after their young very well.

HERE THEY ARE!

IT WOULD BE GREAT IF MY HUSBAND LOOKED AFTER OUR BABIES THAT WELL!

WHO WILL TAKE CARE OF US?

When it comes to animals, fathers usually don't take part in rearing their young. They reproduce with their chosen partner, and then go about their business. Mothers are left to provide all the care, education, and rearing. An exception to this is seahorses – these males carry their young in their pouch until hatching. However, there are animals that divide the care equally among themselves. Penguins, for example, do it quite cleverly. ◄

MEMORIES OF CHILDHOOD

The juvenile stage can last entire years for some animals, for example in the case of chimpanzees, or mere months and weeks. It depends on many factors: how developed the animal is at birth; what environment it lives in; whether a parent or an entire group takes care of it; or what the parents need to teach it before it grows up. For example, baby marsupials are born undeveloped and must spend a significant amount of time in their mother's pouch where they drink milk and grow stronger. On the other hand, baby zebras and giraffes can walk within an hour of being born – otherwise, they'd be unable to survive in the rough savannah! ▶

I LEARNED HOW TO WALK WHEN I WAS EIGHTEEN MONTHS OLD!

WELL, I WAS ABOUT AN HOU OLD.

HOW MANY OF YOU ARE THERE?

The young animal's upbringing often depends on whether the animals live alone or in a group. The solitary ones meet their partner only for mating; otherwise, they live on their own. For example, alligator mums rely only on themselves. Others live in groups and help each other with rearing the young: grandmas, sisters, older brothers, even aunts twice-removed lend a helping hand. That's how elephants, wolves, or meerkats do it – they divide tasks among each other, which protects them from danger. ▼

AND THIS IS MY AUNT WHO TAUGHT ME HOW TO CATCH MYSELF A SNACK...

A skink eats its own eggs

YIKES!

THE APPROACH TO UPBRINGING

Most parents try to teach their offspring everything they'll need once they grow up: how to get food, defend themselves from enemies, or take care of their own young. Some parents, such as chimpanzees or oystercatchers, show their children how to crack a nut or open a shell. Cubs of many predators fight and tease each other to practice fighting and hunting. The main thing is that they keep all these things in mind! ◄

Providing protection

BAD PARENTING?

Not every animal mother is diligent and loving. Some abandon their young as soon as they are born. There are even those who eat their own child! As horrible as this may seem, there's a reasonable explanation for everything. Many young are born developed, with innate instincts that tell them what to do. But sometimes, a baby animal is born at a time when the mum can't get enough food, or is weak and sick and wouldn't survive for long and the parent has to act for the best. ▲

Getting food

Maintaining relationships

EMPEROR PENGUINS
A FAMILY OF GENTLEMEN

When you see these handsome fellows, you should tip your hat - not because they're all dapper in their tuxedos, but because they manage to take care of their young even in the most challenging circumstances, like it's nothing at all. Cold, hunger, enemies - none of that stops them from raising their tiny penguins and properly preparing them to live in the rough Antarctic wilderness.

EVERYBODY OUT!

IT ALL BEGINS WITH AN EGG

When a female penguin lays an egg, she rolls it over to the male's legs and sets out for a very long journey towards the sea. She's starving and can spend up to two months hunting for food. The diligent father stands watch over the egg, in a huddle with other males. When the right time comes, the little penguin hatches. As soon as it's born, it starts **chirping** and wakes up all the unhatched young around. Thanks to this, all little penguins in the entire colony are born almost at once! ◀

THE NANNY

The male becomes a full-time parent. And he takes his role very seriously! When the baby is still in its egg, he keeps the egg nice and warm on his own feet, covering it with the excess skin of his belly so that it doesn't touch the ice-covered ground or get blown upon by the cold wind. Once the baby is born, he feeds it with a **curdy substance** which he has kept in his crop, a muscular pouch off his oesophagus. He joins forces with other males and forms a group with them to keep all young warm. ▶

THAT'S ENOUGH!

CHANGING OF THE GUARDS

When the mother penguin returns, there is a changing of the guards and the father heads out to hunt. Since the male loses almost half of his body weight during the mother's absence, he's looking forward to his trip indeed. Meanwhile, mums give the tiny penguins their first real meal – such as pieces of fish they caught. ▶

BYE BYE!

FAAAAAALIIING!

FIRST STEPS

As soon as the chicks are too big to fit into the mum's brood pouch, they must take a step towards their new life – literally! In order to stretch their legs, they practice walking on the mother's toes at first. They're unstable, just like human toddlers. Fortunately, their furry **down** softens all falls and as they continue practicing, they get better and better at getting around. ◀

MEEE TOOO!

PULLING TOGETHER

After about six months, the young penguins stop receiving their food from their mothers. Time to jump into the **sea**! They slide on their bellies into the water and go hunting alongside their parents. They've learned much from them already, and are great swimmers and divers. Before long, they'll pass on their knowledge to their own children. ▼

Shabby

Shaggy

Swell

PROBLEMS OF ADOLESCENCE

While growing up, penguins change in front of your very eyes. When a penguin is born, it has soft, downy feathers, but before it reaches the slick appearance of an adult emperor penguin, it goes through a period of **moulting**, as each baby feather is replaced with a new adult one. ▲

AMERICAN ALLIGATORS

TOUGH AND TENDER

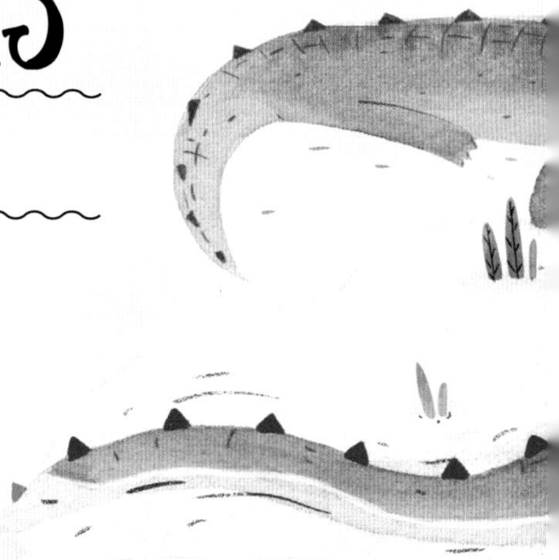

Alligators look like natural tough guys, and they are! After all, they're kind of living fossils - they've been inhabiting the Earth for millions of years, survived dinosaurs and the ice age, and haven't changed very much the entire time. When it comes to children, however, you'd be hard-pressed to find more loving mums. So don't let their armoured back and robust jaws fool you!

SEE YOU LATER, ALLIGATOR...

SINGLE MUM

Alligator **fathers** aren't involved in rearing the young. However, the mother alligator takes on all of the responsibility, taking care of the baby alligators from before the eggs are even laid! ▶

Preparing the nest

LIKE IN A FEATHER BED

Before the mother lays her eggs, she prepares a **nest** for them, sort of like a cradle. She lines it with vegetation and mud to make it comfortable and to hide it from the eyes of enemies. After laying the eggs, she doesn't sit on them like a chicken would, but guards the nest from afar. It can be very dangerous for any animal that approaches an alligator nest! ◀

Chauffeur mother

COMING INTO THIS WORLD

When the time to be hatched comes, the young alligators start making noises that the mum can hear through the shells of their eggs. If the babies don't manage to break through the leathery shell with their pointy **egg tooth**, she rushes at once to help them. ▲

WHY IS YOUR MOUTH SO BIG?

Small alligators are vulnerable, and so their mum must protect them. Even though they're instinctively able to swim from birth, the mum prefers to **put them into her mouth** and carry them to safety. It's good to err on the side of caution, after all! ▼

PRETTY NEAT, HUH?

Proud mum

SAFETY ABOVE ALL

The alligator mother is very protective, and will attack another animal that comes close to her young. Sometimes, she carries the young on her back, or calls them over and hides them inside her mouth. The most important thing is to **protect** them until they're big enough to fend for themselves. ◄

MUM, I'M ALL GROWN UP

Mother alligators look after their young for up to two or three years. Then, the young leave the safe environment of their home and go out to start their own adult lives. Larger males usually find their own territory, while smaller alligators might live in closer proximity to one another. ▲

RED KANGAROOS

WALKING INCUBATORS

These Australian mothers don't just have pockets for no reason. Kangaroos are marsupials - a type of animal that has a pouch to carry their young around in. Apart from this perfect pocket, kangaroos also have strong legs and a tail that help them to move around, mainly by jumping. Kangaroos are very responsible parents - if the conditions are unfavourable (such as a drought, or a lack of food), they hold off on having babies, waiting until a better season for raising young,

Kangaroo incubator

MINI BABY

When a little kangaroo is born, it's about the size of a bean. Even though it's almost **undeveloped** – pink and blind – it climbs up the mother's fur, all the way into the pouch where it stays for several months, like it would in an incubator. It slowly grows there, feeding on the mother's milk until it is large enough to peek out of the pouch. ▲

LET'S PLAY PEEK-A-BOO

When the little kangaroo is about six months old, it carefully peeks out of the pouch, and then starts looking around. After a while, it dares to climb out for a short time. This allows the mum to clean up the pouch a bit and take a rest. However, if she senses danger she'll call the baby over immediately. You can often spot tiny kangaroos with their head hidden in the mum's pouch, either feeding or resting. ▼

ALREADY?

COME ON, TIME TO GO OUT!

Kangaroo's pouch

POCKET PALS

Kangaroo mothers can have another baby even if they have one joey in the pouch already. The mother is able to provide for each of them, even managing to give the baby the **more nutritious** milk it needs, different to what its older sibling receives. Once they're both grown up, the older sibling watches out for the younger one. ▶

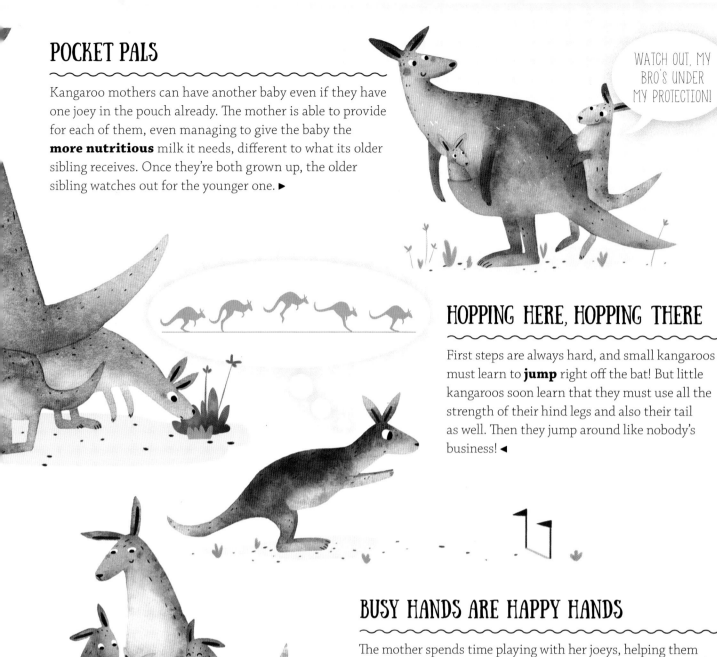

WATCH OUT, MY BRO'S UNDER MY PROTECTION!

HOPPING HERE, HOPPING THERE

First steps are always hard, and small kangaroos must learn to **jump** right off the bat! But little kangaroos soon learn that they must use all the strength of their hind legs and also their tail as well. Then they jump around like nobody's business! ◀

BUSY HANDS ARE HAPPY HANDS

The mother spends time playing with her joeys, helping them develop agility, as well as other social skills. They will play-fight, which can be good training for the future as adult males often '**box**' each other to determine which one of them is the larger and stronger tough guy. ▼

COME CUDDLE UP!

Male kangaroos leave their mother after three or four years, and females usually stay and become super mums themselves. But while they are young enough to live in the pouch, the mother likes to sniff, lick, and cuddle them – a mother and her joeys are a very close family group. ▲

HIYAH!

CHIMPANZEES

PROUD PRIMATE PARENTS

This chimpanzee family isn't too different from human ones. Did you know that primates are similar to us in a lot of respects? There's a 98 per cent similarity of DNA between chimpanzees and humans. And the likeness doesn't end there: they're immensely intelligent, have strong bonds with the other members of the group, and use an elaborate system of communication. And most importantly, chimpanzee mothers look after their babies with great tenderness and spend all their time with them.

Group hierarchy

A NEW ADDITION TO THE FAMILY

When a baby is born to a chimpanzee mum, it's as **vulnerable** as a human one. For the first couple of months, the mum cares for it with a great attention and constantly carries it around on her body. She provides it with protection, food, and keeps it warm at night, as it tends to be cold in the tree tops where they sleep in a nest. Once they cuddle up, it's all well and good. ▼

FAMILY BONDS

Chimpanzees live in large groups where everybody has their designated place. Big males are the most respected of all because they look after the group and guard it. Mothers spend most of their time caring for babies. But older siblings and other relatives aren't left out, either – they often help the mother, play with the others, or maintain friendly relationships by combing the fur of their fellows, looking for a tasty snack. ▲

HUSH, MY BABY...

APE NURSERY

When the baby grows up a bit, the mother carries it around on her **back**. The small chimpanzee ventures outside the mother's company only after about two years. It romps with friends, plays games with them, and learns everything important. However, it still sticks near to its mother, never leaving her sight. ▶

LEARN YOUNG

Chimpanzee mothers teach their young everything they need to know, like how to get food or which herbs to eat when one feels sick. Chimpanzees are **very smart** – they can use a rod to catch termites with, and are able to crack tasty nuts with stones. Just show the young how to go about it, and they'll pull it off themselves next time. ▼

BUSY HANDS ARE HAPPY HANDS

Small chimpanzees are very **playful** – they can climb as early as six months after they're born, and tree branches are their second home. They play about with their friends, but also explore everything around. Every leaf, pebble, even every berry is of interest to them. The older members of the community look after them – after all, it's all fun and games until someone gets hurt. ◀

Excitement

Fear

Consolation

WHAT DID YOU SAY?

Chimpanzees communicate using **sounds, facial expressions, and gestures**. When the group finds food, the members start making noises that the others translate to mean: a goodie is around! You can tell by their facial expression when they're happy, angry, or scared. There are gestures, as well – a friendly pat on the back, a consolation kiss, or an order to commence the scratching. Chimpanzees simply understand one another! ▲

WOW!

Learning by mimicking

MUTE SWANS

A DYNAMIC DUO

This family has it all figured out - mum and dad look after their grey-brown brood equally. Did you know that swan couples stay together until death? Maybe that's why they treat their children with so much affection. Both adults raise them lovingly, teach them everything, and carefully guard them. Swan fathers can really ruffle feathers; it's not a good idea to mess with them, and it doesn't matter whether they're in the middle of a busy park or by a peaceful pond.

BUT I'M NOT YOUR MUM!

Swan's nest

A SWAN IS COMING OVER!

Before the mum lays her eggs, she must make a **bed** for them – a king-size bed, in fact. She uses her strong beak to carry over various twigs, reeds, and other plants so that the eggs are as snug as a bug in a rug – and safe as well! When the mum lays the eggs, usually over the course of five to seven days, she sits on them until they hatch. The dad sometimes takes over, but mostly prefers to watch out and make sure the family stays safe. ▶

IT'S TOO COLD!

WELCOME TO THE WORLD!

Both parents warm the eggs up for about a month until they hatch. And here they come! The shells are starting to crack and tiny grey heads are peeking out of them. Once all the young are **hatched**, they immediately go and cuddle up with the mum – that's how their wet feathers get dry and they can be warm and safe. A well-deserved rest follows. The babies must recharge their batteries – their first swimming lesson awaits them the next day! ◀

I'M KNACKERED

The baby swans, cygnets, can **walk, swim, and eat** immediately after they're born. The day after their birth, the dad gives them their first swimming lesson – and he doesn't take it easy on them! Each time, he covers a longer distance with them than previously so that they get used to the water. Once their energy is depleted, they climb on the mum's back and get a nice ride home, safe from any danger. ▼

WHAT A RIDE!

I'M ON YOUR HEELS

The freshly hatched swans begin to follow around the very first thing they see. That's why their parents try to form as close a **relationship** with them as possible. They even 'talk' to the eggs so that the young can recognise their voices. The parents want to make sure that the babies won't mistake them for just any duck that happens to pass by. As soon as the young hatch, they start carefully observing their parents to learn all important things from them. ◄

JUST SPREAD YOUR WINGS, KIDS, AND WHOOSH. IS IT CLEAR?

THE FIRST DAY OF FLYING

When the cygnets are about six months old, the parents proceed to teach them **how to fly**. At first, though, the young need to diligently stretch their wings and strengthen their chest muscles. When the day comes, the parents show their young an example of how to fly several times, and then the little ones try it for themselves. ▶

SURE THING, DAD!

OFF WITH YOU!

Once the young are about a year old, they're fully **self-sufficient**. When they're almost white, the parents conclude that it's time to lay new eggs – the kids are all grown up, after all! The young are confused at first, but soon find a group of similarly-aged swans to join. Who knows – maybe they'll find their own life-long partner among them to build a nest with... ◄

I'LL WRITE TO YOU!

INDIAN ELEPHANTS

LOVING GIANTS

Elephant calves have it pretty easy. They're taken care of not only by their mums, but also siblings, aunts, and grandmas. That's because they live in a herd led by the eldest cow elephant. The group does almost everything together - the members journey to find food and water, they play together, and maintain familial relationships. The bond between an elephant mum and her calf is one of the strongest you can find in the animal kingdom.

Calf's coming to the world

NO TIME TO WASTE TIME

The freshly born calf can stand on its own legs, walk, and drink the mother's milk only a couple of hours after its birth. Calves are quick learners – they soon join others to journey for food and water, start eating food such as grass, and since they're incredibly smart and curious they start to explore the world around them, most often using their **sensitive trunk** which functions as a sort of a hand. They still stay pretty close to their mother though. ▼

IT'S A CALF, MUM!

A mother elephant has to wait a good long while before her calf is born. She carries the baby in her belly for up to **two years**! When the calf is about to be born, other females gather around the mum, and sometimes even assist her with the delivery. The baby is no mite – elephant calves can weigh up to 100kg. ▲

SPEED UP!

I'M RIGHT ON YOUR HEELS!

WHAT GOOD IS THIS?

It takes a while for the calves to figure out how to use their trunk properly. They look confused during the first week of their life, as if the trunk isn't under their control. They can even trip over it! However, they soon find out how useful it is: they can use it to lift things, spray water into their mouth, shower with it on hot days, use it as a snorkel when they're under water, greet and caress others, trumpet, have conversations… What a truly wonderful thing! ▶

Ways of using the trunk

LITTLE RASCALS

Male juveniles can be proper **rascals**, especially when they turn 12 and reach puberty. They start to take an interest in female elephants and want to show off in front of them. This is why they often nudge other elephants to show them who the boss is. However, their mum or grandma is always nearby to pull their ear. Not too long after that though, they usually leave the female herd, and either wander around alone, or join together with other youths. ◀

BUSY HANDS ARE HAPPY HANDS

Elephant calves spend a lot of time **discovering** the world around them and playing various games. They're just like you – they like to play tag, splash water on one another, even throw sticks. They nudge each other and 'fight' imagined enemies. ▼

PHEW!

FOR EVER AND EVER

Elephant girls usually stay in their own herd until they die. Elephant cows simply pull together: they protect each other, learn how to take care of the young, and if necessary, are always there to help. Calves can **get stuck** in mud or fall into a pit. If that happens, they need their mum, grandma, or aunts to help them out. ▲

HA-HA!

GIRAFFES

LITTLE GIANTS

These elegant, camouflaged giants run around African savannahs, grazing on tiny leaves. The young are looked after mostly by their mothers, who provide them with everything they need: from milk and protection to the life lessons that allow them to survive in the savannah. Even though they're born tall (baby giraffes can have a height of six feet at birth), they still need their mothers!

I'M FALLING!

A giraffe mother carries the baby in her belly for more than a year, leading up to a rough delivery. Giraffes give birth while standing, so the baby starts its life by falling – it drops from the mother at a height of up to about 2m. As soon as it's out, the mother welcomes it by licking and cleaning it. ▼

From such great heights

WHERE'S THE INSTRUCTION MANUAL?

FIRST STEPS

Life is tough on giraffe babies – that's how things are in the savannah. After the initial fall, new trials are waiting just around the corner – the young have to learn to stand on their own legs and go to their mother for a drink of milk. Approximately an hour after its birth, the little giraffe **stands up on its own**. Its steps are wobbly, but don't worry – it will take less than a day for the tiny giraffe to start running! ▶

TIME FOR A SNACK

A giraffe baby lives off its mother's milk for about half a year. After that, it starts looking around and noticing what she eats. Giraffes usually feast on juicy **acacia leaves**. They spend almost the entire day grazing – it's hard work to fill your stomach when you're this tall. The young need to eat a lot in order to quickly grow up. The choicest morsels always grow all the way up at the top of the tree! ▶

YOU CAN'T REACH YET!

ENEMY AT THE GATES!

Any **lion** or **hyena** would love to have giraffe babies for dinner! It's a good thing that the mums have such a long neck – they can spot danger from afar. That's why they chase the young into tall grass to hide. The kids then watch from there to see how they themselves will fight off enemies once they're old enough. Mums know how to kick predators with their long legs – and rest assured, it hurts a bunch. ▼

IN THE NURSERY

When the giraffe babies are a little bit older, the mothers will gather all of the little ones together, and go off alone to graze nearby. The kids play with each other, run around, and pull various pranks. The boys play at 'wrestling' with their long necks. These are the first lessons for their future independent life in the savannah. For now, though, the mothers are still discreetly watching from the distance. ▼

OUCH!

AND DON'T YOU EVER COME BACK!

SEE YOU, THEN

When they're about two years old, the young giraffes are sufficient enough that they no longer need their mothers' help. Why should they? Now they're the **tallest animals** around! Their mother has taught them everything they'll need to know in life. The males become independent and go their own way while the females hang around the herd a little while longer. ▶

SEE YOU AT SATURDAY'S LUNCH?

EUROPEAN CUCKOOS
THE LAZIEST PARENTS OF ALL

Have you ever wondered why it's European cuckoos that are generally called the laziest parents? It's because they don't look after their young at all and leave the privilege to others - bird foster parents they selected earlier. A cuckoo's parental duties end with laying the eggs. After the mum is done, she sets out for a long journey to the warm, African wilderness with a clear conscience. This makes cuckoos an obvious candidate for the Worst Parent of the Year award!

I'LL WARM YOU UP REALLY WELL SO THAT YOU'RE AHEAD!

GLIMMERS OF PARENTHOOD

Most birds enjoy parenthood – they build a nest, put their valuable eggs in it, and take care of them until the young hatch. However, cuckoos chose **the path of least resistance**. That doesn't mean, though, that they don't think about the future of their children. Quite on the contrary! Although they leave their eggs soon and leave the upbringing to others, they still try to instil everything important in their children and provide them with prosperity. In the tropics, you can even encounter distant relatives of the cuckoo genus that look after their young in an exemplary fashion. ▼

I WONDER HOW JUNIOR IS DOING.

A SECURE FUTURE

Before the female lays her eggs, she maps the territory and selects a good nest to put her eggs in. Most often, she picks **the open nests** of small insect-eating songbirds because those are just right for this covert mission. To make sure the operation succeeds, she makes sure that her child is the first one to hatch in the nest. How does she do it? For about a day, she carries the egg in her body like in an incubator, and warms it up as if she were sitting on it. This gives the tot a one-day head start on the foster parents' own young. ▲

EGG FOR AN EGG

Cuckoos always lay only one egg into the nest they have selected. Step number one: maintain the number of eggs. To make sure that the owner of the nest doesn't become suspicious, the mum throws one of the original eggs out and replaces it with one of her own. Step number two: camouflage. Cuckoos choose foster parents whose eggs resemble their own. Even though a cuckoo egg is a little larger, it has a similar colour. Step number three: make a bolt for it. The whole exchange happens very quickly – sometimes it lasts only 10 seconds! ▶

DONE! I'LL BE OFF, THEN.

A LITTLE GANGSTER

Thanks to the head start provided by its mum, the cuckoo young hatches first. It may have inherited its cunning senses from its parents – even though it is born blind and bare, it can exert a great force, **throw the other eggs** out of the nest, and thus keep all the food supply for itself – nobody is going to eat from its plate! ◀

WHAT A TOUGH JOB!

MUM, I'M SO HUNGRY!

Little cuckoos are quite **the mouth to feed**. Although they receive all the food that would otherwise support the entire nest, it's not enough. They beg their foster parents for food, peep loudly, and demand another tasty morsel. No wonder that the nest is soon too small for them and they become larger than their foster parent! The cuckoo lets the foster parent feed it even after it reaches adulthood. ▶

HOW DOES A CUCKOO BECOME A CUCKOO?

How do cuckoos know what to do if they aren't raised by their own parents? It may seem incredible but they figure everything out **by instinct**. After leaving the nest, they fly to faraway Africa to spend the winter there – no advice from those who are older and more experienced! Once they return, they follow the same method of child rearing as their folks. ◀

Little cuckoo leaving the nest

POISON DART FROGS

THE EXCEPTION THAT PROVES THE RULE

These multi-coloured frogs differ from other frogs in more ways than just their beautiful colouration. Most frogs lay eggs, leave them immediately, and no longer think about them. Not poison dart frogs, though! They look after their eggs diligently and lovingly. What a rarity among amphibians!

I'M SO EXCITED!

LOOK AT OUR BABIES!

Happy frog couple

MOVING

As soon as **tadpoles** hatch from the eggs, the frog parents are up to their ears in work. As you know, siblings often squabble. And if that isn't enough, poison dart frog siblings are capable of eating each other! That's why the parents put them on their back and carry them to a new home, one after another. It's quite the climb – like if a human parent walked up the stairs all the way to the roof of a skyscraper with their baby. ▼

WELCOME TO THE WORLD

The males of the poison dart frog 'flirt' with their sweethearts, using their **beautiful singing voice**. The sound carries throughout the tropical rainforest and cannot be missed. The female that likes the song sets out in the direction of where it's coming from – a new couple is formed! The pair celebrates their love with a dance, after which the female lays eggs in wet leaves. The dad isn't idle either – he brings water to the eggs so that they stay wet, or simply pees on them. And he watches over them closely. ▲

COOL PLACE!

DINNER TIME!

Parents visit the tots in their tiny **rooms** each day. The mum brings them food because the tadpoles would be hard-pressed to find food for themselves this high up. This means that the parents have to constantly travel up and down, again and again. But what wouldn't a loving mum do for her offspring? ▶

BREAKFAST!

Tadpole's room

Frog's development

I'M GROWING AND GETTING STRONGER

A frog's development is strange indeed: a small egg turns into a legless tadpole, but as it grows, it gradually develops all limbs until it finally starts resembling a frog. What a wonderful transformation – who would have originally thought that the young would really look like its parents in the end? Tadpoles develop into frogs over about two months, but it takes approximately a year for them to become as big as their parents. ◀

SHE'S MINE!!

DO YOU THINK IT WILL TAKE AFTER ME?

Although poison dart frogs are tiny, it's not a good idea to mess with them. They let us and other animals know this with their bright colouration, which means one thing: don't eat me, I'm **poisonous**! But small tadpoles are neither poisonous nor colourful. They don't need to be afraid, however: as they grow, they become not only tinged, but also as toxic as their parents. ▼

DO YOU THINK IT WILL TAKE AFTER ME?

ADULTS

Within a year, the little eggs turn into beautiful frogs. The males carefully guard their territory – any other male that approaches must be ready for a great **frog fight**! And of course, this fight doesn't escape the attention of family-coveting ladies. Let the courtship begin! ▲

WEDDEL SEALS
COLD HARDY FAMILY

Life in frozen Antarctica is not a walk in the park - only truly tough animals manage to survive there. But this adorable family has it all figured out. Its members aren't afraid of the cold and ice; on the contrary - they use them to their advantage. However, the young need to learn how to do so as early as possible. That's why they grow up fast, get stronger, and learn everything necessary from their mum. They live in Antarctica virtually throughout the year, and so ice and snow become a part of their family as well.

I'LL BE BACK IN SHAPE IN NO TIME.

LIKE IN A FREEZER

The mum carries her young in her belly for almost a year. The newborn must be really shocked when it's born and falls out of the warm belly right into the snow and ice – it must be like being shoved into a freezer! The young don't yet have **subcutaneous fat** that would protect them from the cold, so they must quickly start drinking the mother's milk. They get fatter gradually, but at least they have shaggy fur from the very beginning to keep them warm. ▼

Nutritious milk

I WANT TO GO BACK TO GET WARM!

GETTING FATTER AND STRONGER

Seal milk is **very nutritious**; it's up to 60 per cent fat! Just for comparison – cow milk is only about 4 per cent fat. No wonder, then, that the tots soon become proper busters. They have a lot of catching up to do, after all – when they are born, their flippers are too big and the young need to grow into them. The little seals look hilarious while flipping about on the ice, but after a couple of weeks of hearty nutrition they can weigh up to twice as much as when they were born! The mum, meanwhile, gets slimmer as she feeds the young. Well, anything for the kids! ▲

A FLIPPER HERE, A FLIPPER THERE

After the first week, the mum starts teaching the small seal how to swim. After all, it will spend the most of its life **under water**. The young often have no idea what they should be doing in the water. Should they stick a flipper in it? Their head? The mum usually decides to go for a shock treatment – she simply shoves the baby right into the water. As soon as the young realises that it can swim under the surface if it holds its breath, it's easy going. ▶

LIFE UNDER THE WATER

After approximately five weeks, the young stops drinking its mother's milk. It's high time for the baby to learn how to catch itself a snack. Seals are natural-born **swimmers** and **divers**. They can stay under the water for at least 45 minutes on one breath, and can dive really deep. However, they mustn't forget to hollow out a breathing hole in the ice – they come back to it every time they need to take a breath. They cut it into the ice with their teeth, which is why the young already have their teeth from birth. ◀

HELLO?

Did you know that seal families like to **talk** to one another? The mum and her pup always recognise each other. When the tot withdraws from its mum surreptitiously, she knows how to call it back. Their conversations are so loud they can be heard even when the family is swimming under the ice! ▶

YEAH, MUM, I SWEAR: I'VE ALREADY PRACTICED MY HUNTING TODAY!

HAVEN'T WE MET ALREADY?

HELLO, BEAUTY!

As soon as the pup is **self-sufficient**, the mum goes out to find a new partner to have another baby with. She's already passed the most important lessons on to her child – the pup can swim and cut its own breathing hole in the ice. There's only one thing left for it to do – find a partner to start its own family with. ◀

MEERKATS

A LARGE FAMILY

Just picture it - a meerkat family, that's not just a mum, dad, and their babies. It includes all the grandmas, grandpas, aunts, uncles, and other distant relatives. Meerkats live in large groups where every member has a role. The group is led by the mum who gives birth to the young. However, she's not the only one taking care of them - everyone lends a helping hand and is happy to do so. After all, they know there's strength in numbers.

Underground maze

PLAYING HIDE-AND-SEEK

Meerkats retreat to **underground burrows** where they're protected from enemies and the rough desert weather. The whole group lives there. It's spacious enough, with many chambers that serve different purposes – bedrooms, bathrooms, even a room where meerkat babies are born. The newborns are blind, bare, and defenceless, which is why it's best for them to stay hidden until they grow up a bit. ▲

SUPERVISORS

When the young are about three weeks old, they venture outside the dark underground for the very first time and peek out to see the sun. They don't go too far from the burrow, though, and there's always an adult who **watches over them**. If there's any danger lurking around, the adult takes the young inside his or her mouth and carries them back to safety. ▼

The first time out

LIFE OUTSIDE

The young get slowly used to a life outside the burrow. They find out that when they start whining, the others will pay closer attention to them and bring them food. As the young drink their mother's milk, they gradually begin also accepting the food they'll be **hunting** for later in life. ▼

PLAYING AND LEARNING

Just like other young, meerkats love to **play**. They're very curious animals. The boys like to fight and they view it as a practice for the future. When the time comes that they have to defend their own territory, the skills will come in handy. The young also often experiment with what can and can't be eaten – they chew on twigs as well as pebbles. And as always, there's an adult supervisor watching over them. ▼

JUST BE CAREFUL.

IT'S YOUR TURN!

OOH-LA-LA!

Cleaning the fur

Getting food

Standing on the hind legs

DAY BY DAY

A year after the young are born, they're adults and become full-fledged members of the community. They follow a **daily routine**: get up, go outside, warm their belly, divide tasks among themselves, and go find a tasty snack. Someone stands guard so that he or she can warn the group against enemies. Others watch over the young. Together, they manage to do everything, even chasing off a snake! ▼

ESSENTIAL KNOWLEDGE

Once meerkats are big, they start going outside with their group, hunting for food, watching over others, and act as a nanny for the newly arrived young. That's why it's so important for them to **learn** everything: standing on one's hind legs, for example, is no laughing matter and requires good balance. One's fur doesn't become free of parasites by itself, either. However, learning is exhausting and must be punctuated by short naps. ▲

TIME TO SUNBATHE!

SEAHORSES
A DIFFERENT KIND OF PARENT

Seahorses are peculiar creatures - their head looks like a horse's head, their tail like a monkey's tail. However, they're actually fish! Seahorses differ from other fish not only in appearance, but in behaviour as well. They're slow swimmers, have an erect body, and - most uniquely - are one of the few species where males and females switch the usual parental roles: it's the father, not the mother, who carries the young in his belly. That's why seahorses are often called a shining example of parenthood. But is it deserved?

WHEN A BOY LIKES A GIRL

Before two seahorses decide to have a baby, they perform a little mating **dance** to make sure their bond is strong enough. After the dance is over, the female lays eggs into her partner's belly pouch. The male fertilises them and carries the eggs in his pouch until they're mature enough to hatch. Because there's a lot of them (the female can lay hundreds of eggs), his belly is pretty full. ▶

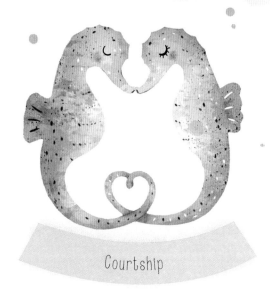

Courtship

LOOK AT YOU!

NO TWO POUCHES ARE ALIKE

The seahorse takes good care of his eggs by bringing **oxygen** to them, and gradually **salt water** as well. Why? To make them prepared for the outside world once they're born. The mum checks up on the male daily: just to make sure. When the tots are born, they leave the dad's pouch for good. It's not the same case as kangaroo joeys – once the seahorses are out of the pouch, they stay out. ◀

28

RUN FOR YOUR LIVES!

LOOKING AFTER THE YOUNG

Do you think that the dad takes care of the newborn little horses as diligently as when he was carrying them around in his pouch? Sadly, no. When the little horses are born, they're fully **developed** and **self-sufficient**. Nobody will look after them ever again, which is why a new rule takes hold: "It's every man for himself!" ◀

IT'S UP TO YOU

Seahorses must watch out for predators and strong ocean currents, too. The baby seahorses can be carried away by a current in a jiffy. However, they are not entirely defenceless. They have **armour** (bone plates on their skin), a **proboscis** (a small mouth at the end of their snout that they use to suck in food, like one would with a vacuum cleaner), and a **prehensile tail** with which they can anchor themselves to a coral or their partner. ▶

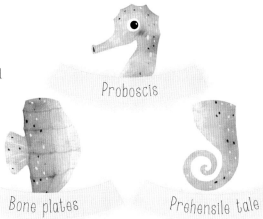

Proboscis

Bone plates

Prehensile tale

AGAIN AND AGAIN

Seahorse dads are really **devoted** to their lifelong task. As soon as they let the babies out into the world, they start looking for a female to have new children with. It's necessary, though – although seahorses can give birth to hundreds of offspring at a time, only about 20 per cent of them manage to survive the tough underwater world. ▼

I'M ALL GROWN UP, TOO!

When a male horse grows up – essentially, reaching the size of its parents – he can consider himself an adult, since he has successfully overcome all the dangers lurking under the surface of the sea. It's time to move on in life, find a partner, get pregnant, and release a new generation of tiny seahorses into the world. This process is needed because the number of seahorses is **constantly decreasing** – unfortunately, humans are destroying their natural environment or hunt them too much, for example for decoration. ◀

MATERNITY LEAVE IS OVER. TIME TO MAKE MORE TOTS!

BLACK-BACKED JACKALS

A FAITHFUL FAMILY

These canine predators could serve as an example to other animals. The way they look after their family is simply incredible. The upbringing of the young is equally divided between the mum and dad. Even older siblings pitch in! One can survive the rough African savannah only by working together. The more jackal family members that take part in the upbringing, the higher the chance that the next generation will greatly increase in numbers.

A couple in love

AN UNUSUAL COUPLE

Jackal couples in love faithfully stand side by side for **their entire life**. This is something one doesn't encounter very often in the wilderness. The partners are well coordinated and both of them take diligent care of their children. If they didn't, they wouldn't be able to raise more and more generations of little jackals. ◀

COSY HOME

The mum gives birth in the safety of her house: an **underground burrow**. She can have up to nine little jackal pups! To make sure they're all safe, they spend several weeks in the burrow. Since the pups are blind and toothless, the mum nurses, protects, and warms them up. Because she rarely leaves her kingdom, the dad must lend a helping hand and get her something good to eat. ▶

DELIVERY SERVICE!

YAY!

TIME TO PLAY

When they grow up a bit, the pups go **outside the burrow** to explore. At first, they cautiously stick their muzzle out, but soon are fearlessly discovering the outside world. Pups love to play and can do so for hours: they tease each other, jump around, fight and play tag. They develop their muscles in this way, but also acquire the necessary experience they'll rely on once they reach adulthood. ▼

SUPER DAD

It doesn't take long for the pups to want something more nutritious to eat than their mother's milk. That's when the dad's time to shine comes: not only can he get food for the entire family, but he also tidies up, licks the pups clean, spends his time playing with them and protecting them. What a **super dad**, right? ◄

YOUNG ADULTS

Jackals often get help from their **older siblings**. When they grow up, they stay with their parents for about six months, even though they could start their own family already. Why do they do this? By staying at home for longer than is strictly necessary, they gain protection, can practice hunting or defence against enemies more, and learn to look after the young. When the young adults are about 18 months old, they're experienced and confident enough to move away from their parents. ▼

MUM, I'M THIRSTY!

A HARMONIC COHABITATION

Jackals simply have it all figured out. When the whole family **pulls together**, everybody benefits. The parents don't have to worry for the little ones, the young adults learn to take care of pups, and the youngest ones learn and come to know everything they need. ◄

Happy jackal family

WILD RABBITS

ABSENTEE PARENT

Just look at this load of adorable furry fellows who laze about in their comfortable warm nest. The nest was prepared by their mum so that the little rabbits would stay warm and safe. But wait, where is the mum going? Hello, Mrs. Rabbit, don't you want to spend time with your tots?

I'M NO YOUNG TOFF!

ANY RESEMBLANCE IS PURELY COINCIDENTAL

Do you think that wild rabbits resemble your cute pets? It's no wonder if you do: wild rabbits are the **ancestors** of all domestic rabbit breeds. But unlike our cute playmates they're much more **self-sufficient**. They're nocturnal, very social animals that live in colonies, in complex underground burrows. ◄

I RECKON THAT'S SOFT ENOUGH.

BUNNY BABIES GALORE

The female rabbit has young **several times** a year, from spring to winter. Yearly, she can give birth to up to 30 adorable babies! This means she doesn't spend a long period of time raising each group of young. The male doesn't help at all. Before the mum gives birth, she prepares a bed for the tots and lines it with dry grass, moss, and fur she plucks from her own belly. The newborns will be as snug as a bug in a rug! ▶

A MAN'S HOME IS HIS CASTLE

The complex system of **underground burrows** is occupied by several rabbit families at once. Let me tell you, it's quite a maze. The burrows have several entrances, tunnels, and emergency exits. The older females inhabit the main 'castle' while the lower-status females build short dens at the edge to house their young in. They're often disguised with grass so that the entrance stays hidden from enemies. ▼

Rabbit burrow

SAFETY ABOVE ALL

Rabbits are a delicacy to foxes, badgers, or weasels. That's why the mum leaves the tiny rabbits in the burrow once they're born, and runs away. She returns to see and feed them only twice a day: at dawn and dusk. The entire meeting lasts just about five minutes, and then the mum dashes off once again. This is the only way to make sure that she doesn't leave her **scent** in the burrow, which might attract enemies to the little rabbits. ▲

A LONELY ADOLESCENCE

Since the young are born bare and blind, they are **easy prey** for all cunning predators. It may seem cruel of the mum to leave her young alone, but it is for the best. And since her milk is very nutritious, the tiny rabbits soon grow up. After three weeks, they're big and self-sufficient enough to do without their mum. ▶

I CAN DO IT BY MYSELF

The grown-up young are **well equipped** to deal with the outside world: they have long, erect ears that detect all imminent danger. They can hop to get away from enemies, and find their own food. They're also instinctively able to hide from predators. What else would one need? When they're four months old, they can already start a large rabbit family of their own. ◀

HONEYBEES

ONE LARGE FAMILY

Insects usually aren't fans of rearing their young. Bees are one of the few exceptions. You'd be hard-pressed to find a larger family than theirs. Beehives house thousands of bees that live in well-organised colonies. This family works like a well-oiled machine: everyone has their task and tries to fulfil it to the best of their ability. That's why a bee family grows very quickly! To find out the secret behind this great family dynamic, we must look inside. Let's go for a visit, then!

Queen

Worker bee

Drone

WHO IS WHO IN THE BEEHIVE?

Each bee colony has a queen or a mother. Only the queen can lay eggs – sometimes up to 1500 a day! **Worker bees** hatch from most of them. These bees do all the work. Some of them, though, can evolve into new queens. There are unfertilised eggs, too, from which drones hatch. Drones live only short lives since their only mission is to have babies with the queen. ◄

WHAT DOES A BEE HOME LOOK LIKE?

Inside a beehive is honeycomb, a structure made from watertight hexagonal cells. These chambers serve different purposes: some of them function as honey storerooms and are used mainly in winter when there's a lack of blossoms and nectar. Inside the most interesting chambers, **larvae develop**. This is where worker bees take diligent care of eggs and larvae to produce new bees! ►

SWEET DREAMS.

PHEW, THAT WAS HARD!

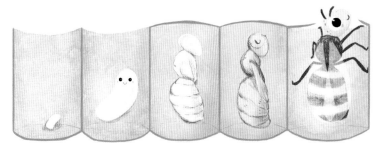

FROM AN EGG TO A BEE

After three days, a larva hatches from the laid egg. Its older sisters – the worker bees – feed it the most nutritious food that can be found in the beehive: **royal jelly**, which makes the larvae grow, fatten up, and get stronger. After six days of being intensively fattened up, they're thousands of times bigger than before! Larvae in the queen cells – the largest cells in the honeycomb where future queens hatch – are fed most of all. Then, the fattened larvae enter the pupa stage in their lidded cell. After about twelve days when the young bees are large enough, they bite their way out. ▲

QUEEN BEE

The queen's mission is to **lay eggs**. That's her sole job. She's surrounded by helpers – worker bees – who feed and clean her, make her comfortable, and generally ensure that she can focus on her main task. The queen bee works full time and lays eggs all day. Nobody can take over for her so it's no wonder that she's treated like a royal. ◄

FUTURE OCCUPATION

s soon as the bees hatch, they become a **part of he colony** and get assigned a job. Worker bees are he largest group in any beehive since they have nany functions: first, they clean up the cells of the oneycomb, then they feed the young, build new cells, ir out the beehive, collect pollen, guard the beehive... hew, being born a worker bee isn't all sweetness nd light. ▼

MOVING AWAY

When bees reproduce, it's called **swarming**. The bee colony divides in two parts: one group, led by a queen, flies away to find a new hollow and build new honeycomb. The other group stays in the beehive where the new queen was born. I bet it has never occurred to you there are so many kingdoms in the world! ▲

See you next time!

WHY KANGAROOS
HAVE POCKETS
HOW ANIMALS CARE FOR THEIR YOUNG

© Designed by B4U Publishing, 2018
member of Albatros Media Group
Author: Pavla Hanáčková
Illustrator: Linh Dao
All rights reserved.

Published by Australian Geographic
52–54 Turner Street, Redfern, NSW 2016
www.australiangeographic.com.au
Australian Geographic customer service
1300 555 176 (local call rate within Australia)